Army Ant Parade

APRIL PULLEY SAYRE

ILLUSTRATED BY RICK CHRUSTOWSKI

HENRY HOLT AND COMPANY

NEW YORK

If you awake in a tent
under a green canopy of trees
one morning in Panama,
and all you hear is your heartbeat
and a strange silence,
then you will know they are coming.

Fee-few a bird calls.
Shapes flutter. Flies buzz.
These are good signs. Hope for more.
Tuck your pant legs into your socks.
Be bold and quiet. And look for birds
with blue-ringed eyes.

Churr, cheerr, chirrrrrrrrr. The birds twitter and trill.
Is there a rustling, like rattling rain?
If so, then move closer. Watch where you step.
Check tree limbs, leaves, and logs.
Chew-chew-chew an antbird calls. Shapes flit.
A grasshopper thumps into a trunk.
Thwap, pip, pop. Insects leap up, jump up, fly up!
Scorpions scurry. Something is happening!

Frogs are hopping. Tarantulas are scampering.
Snakes are slithering away.
Could it be what you hoped?

Yes! The army ants are waking . . .
and they are coming right this way!
A living ball of ants is breaking and spreading.
Army ants swarm over the leaves and dirt.
You, and only you, are going to witness
one of the greatest spectacles on earth.

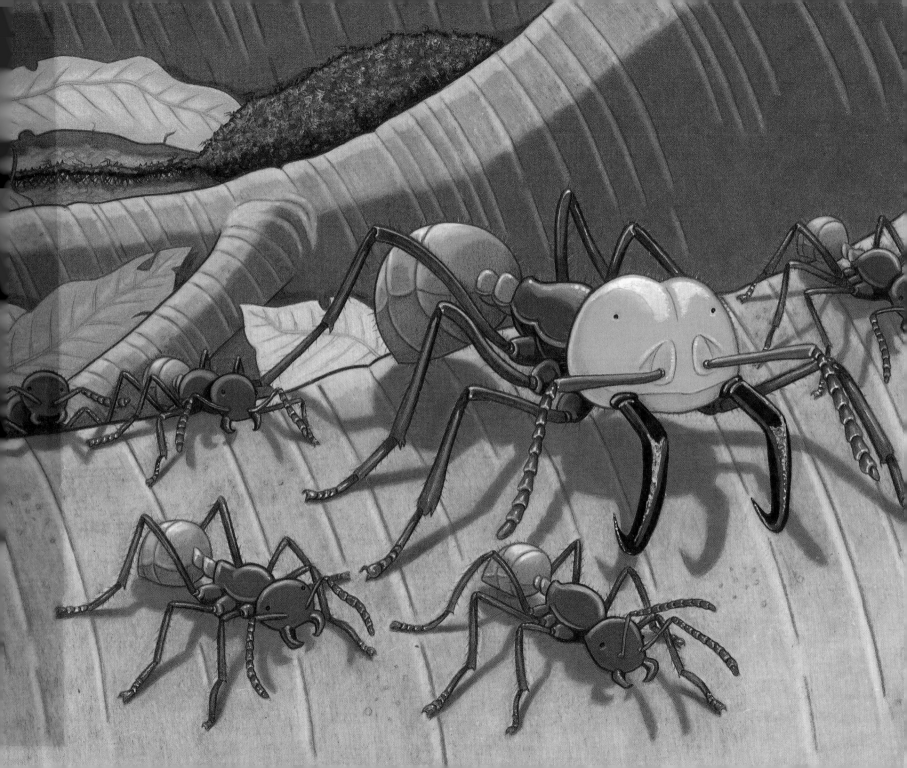

First a trickle,
then a stream,
then a river of ants flows outward,
flooding the forest floor.
Small and medium-sized ants
push forward, hunting for food.
Big soldier ants hug the sides.

Are you standing in the swarm? Don't run. Just step aside.
Ants may march up your boots—but not far.
The army ant parade is here!
Look for antbirds hopping in the swarm.

Chew-chew-chew-chew-cheep-cheep-cheep-cheep.
Antbirds don't eat the ants. Ants taste bad.
Antbirds snatch and swallow the many insects
stirred up by the swarm.

Buzz, zizz, buzz. Tachinid flies follow, too,
laying eggs on the insects that flee.
Lizards skirt the edges, grabbing fleeing insects.
Butterflies drink droppings antbirds leave.

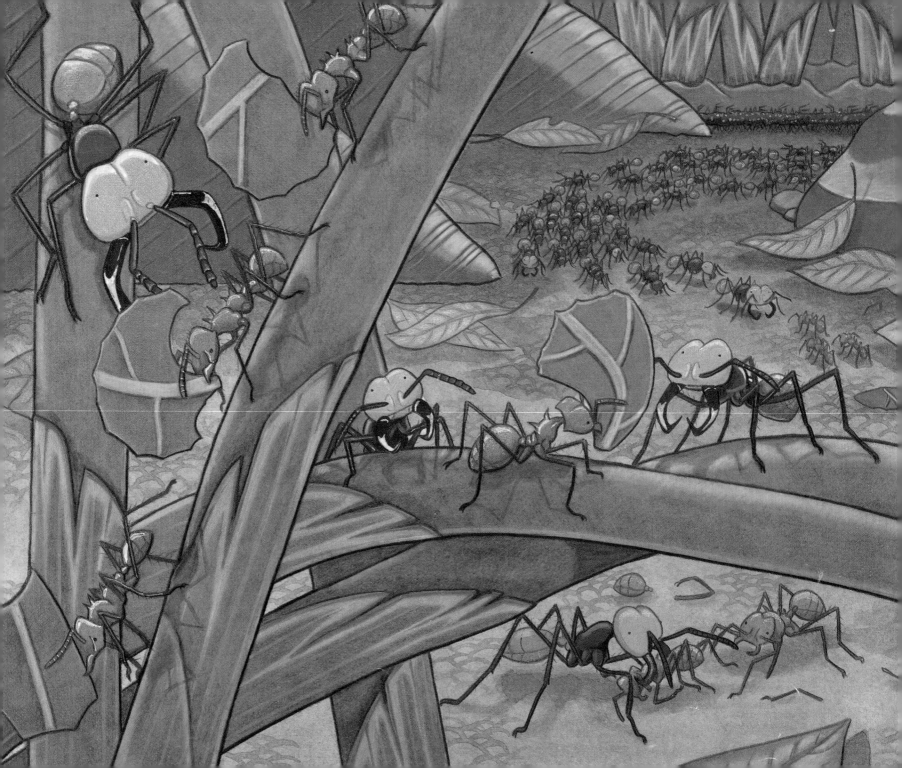

Look! Leaf cutter ants are doing battle, defending their nest.

A frog is caught in the swarm and hops too late.
The ants catch it. There are many ants to feed.
A mother bird peers out from her cozy nest.
Her chicks can't fly. And ants are climbing closer. . . .

Quick! Snap, snap! She picks off the ants.
Her chicks nestle down, safe and snug.
Feee, few-few-few-few. Churr, chack, chip! Buzz, zizz, buzz.
The rustling, bustling swarm moves along.

Stick insects stand oh-so-perfectly still,
hidden from the hungry throng.
With green leafy wings, a katydid blends in.
But when it moves, the ants see it. Up it flies.
Bark-brown beetles helicopter higher.
A howler monkey watches, wide-eyed.

Soon the ant swarm has passed.
No more leaves rustling
or flies buzzing.
No more insects fleeing, *thwap, pip, pop!*
All is quiet in the forest again—
except for the beating of your heart.

MORE ABOUT ARMY ANTS

Army ants march through the rain forests and dry forests of Central and South America. At dawn, the ants swarm through the forests looking for food. They kill and eat other insects, spiders, and scorpions. Lizards, frogs, snakes, small birds, and mice caught in their path may be killed as well.

Most animals scatter to escape the ants, but some insect eaters follow the swarms. Insects can be hard to see. They hide under bark or tree leaves. Many blend into their surroundings. But when army ants sweep through the forest, hidden insects fly, hop, or run away, making them easy to find. Various species of antbirds, antthrushes, antwrens, and tanagers follow the army ants to catch the fleeing insects. But they usually don't eat the ants because the ants taste bad to them. Only woodcreepers, which are bark-colored birds, consume a lot of ants.

Tachinid (TA-keh-nehd) flies follow ant swarms to lay eggs on the insects that fly up or run away. When the eggs hatch, the larvae kill and eat the insects. The last of the followers are the ithomiine (ee-toe-me-EE-nay) butterflies, which feed on antbird droppings.

The ant swarm comes from a ball of ants under a log, against a tree, or inside a tree trunk. The ants lock their legs and bodies together to form this ball, which is called a bivouac. The bivouac protects the queen and the larvae. The swarming ants bring pieces of prey back to the bivouac via a narrow two-way ant highway. At night, the ants that swarmed return to the bivouac. Or they start a new bivouac and carry the larvae to it. After two weeks, the larvae make cocoons for themselves and become pupae, and the bivouac hides inside a tree for three weeks until the new ants emerge. During this time, the ants don't swarm every day because there are no larvae to feed. When another group of eggs hatches, the ants will swarm again.

Central and South American army ants pose very little threat to humans. Their bites and stings are no more harmful than those of other small ants. Although they sometimes climb up boots, army ants rarely attack through clothing. But most people step aside, just in case. Besides, it's easier to get good views of the antbirds if you stay out of the way of the swarm.

To Jeff, ant follower extraordinaire! —*A. P. S.*

To my family—we march through life together. —*R. C.*

ACKNOWLEDGMENTS

Many thanks to the following people: Dr. Edwin O. Willis reviewed portions of this text; he and his wife, Yoshika Oniki, carried out the scientific research that formed a background for this book. Antbird researcher Dr. Gene Morton gave us helpful comments. Raúl Arias de Para was our gracious host at the canopy tower in Panama; guides Carmen Martino and Edwin Miranda helped us find army ant swarms.

A portion of the author's proceeds from this book goes to tropical bird research and conservation, through the grant program of the American Bird Conservancy, P.O. Box 249, The Plains, VA 20198. You can find out more about this not-for-profit conservation group at: www.abcbirds.org.

Henry Holt and Company, LLC, *Publishers since 1866*
115 West 18th Street, New York, New York 10011

Library of Congress Cataloging-in-Publication Data
Sayre, April Pulley.
Army ant parade / April Pulley Sayre; illustrations by Rick Chrustowski.
1. Army ants—Juvenile literature. [1. Army ants. 2. Ants.]
I. Chrustowski, Rick, ill. II. Title.
QL568.F7 S29 2002   595.79'6—dc21   2001000285

ISBN 0-8050-6353-6
First Edition—2002 / Book design by David Caplan
Printed in the United States of America on acid-free paper. ∞

10 9 8 7 6 5 4 3 2 1

The artist used up to forty layers of colored pencil over watercolor wash on 140-pound watercolor paper to create the illustrations for this book.